Handy Crafts FROM Scraps

Handy Crafts
FROM Scraps

*A Collection of Illustrated How-To-Make Articles
from Scrap and Inexpensive Materials*

by OLIVE HOWIE

*Photos Contributed by Vickie Gale,
Oscar Faulk and Frank Howman*

Publishers
T. S. DENISON & COMPANY, INC.
Minneapolis

DON'T THROW IT AWAY

Many useful and decorative items can be made from articles that are often thrown away. Such things as plastic bottles, coat hangers, cardboard tubing, old hose, boxes, etc., are suitable to use in arts and crafts classes.

The following pages will give you directions for making a number of items. Since the basic materials are discards, these are inexpensive to make.

Many other useful articles can be made from discards, so "put on your thinking cap" and work out some original ideas of your own.

CONTENTS

GIRL'S PURSE

Materials:

Half-gallon plastic container*

Felt (eight inches wide and twelve inches long)

Pair of shoestrings

Cutting tool

Scissors

Ticket punch or ice pick

Glue

Stapler

Procedure:

Scallop bottom edge of felt. This may be marked with a pencil, using a spool or other round object as a pattern. Sew together using an overcast stitch.

Punch ten holes equally spaced two thirds of an inch from the top edge of the felt.

Cut plastic container down to three and a half inches from the bottom.

Slip felt on the plastic container to a depth of one and a half inches. Staple in place. Felt may be glued in place if stapler is not available.

Glue a row of contrasting rickrack on felt top to cover staples and give added color.

A circle of fabric or felt may be glued in the bottom of the purse if desired.

Insert the shoestrings in the holes in the top of the purse from opposite sides so that when they are pulled, the purse will close. Tie a knot in the ends of the strings.

*Since all half-gallon containers may not be the same distance around, you should measure your container to get the correct length of felt.

9

BIRD CAGE

Materials:

Quart-sized plastic bottle

One yard of rickrack

Small lump of modeling clay

Enamel

Cutting tool

Small bird

Permanent flowers

Ruler or piece of straight cardboard

Glue

Procedure:

Draw cutting lines with a ruler or piece of cardboard. Measure your bottle and make evenly spaced lines around the bottle. These lines should be about half an inch apart. With a cutting tool, make vertical slits on these lines down to one inch from the bottom of the bottle. Cut out every other section, leaving openings around the bottle to give a cage effect. Press down on the top of the bottle and the plastic spokes will bend out to make rounded sides.

Glue two rows of rickrack around the top and one around the bottom. If there is any lettering around the bottle, it can be covered with the rickrack.

Put a small lump of clay in the bottom of the cage. Wire bird to stem or wire and stick into the clay. Add enough small flowers to cover the clay. Paint the bottle cap to match the rickrack.

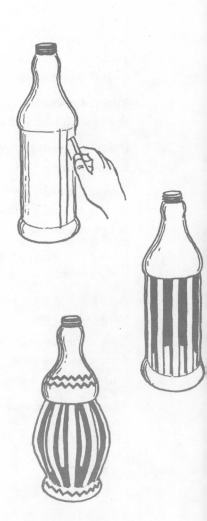

SEWING BASKET

Materials:

One gallon plastic container
Bottom of another container (gallon)
Red or other colored felt
Rickrack to match the felt
Cotton or other stuffing material
Five inches of small wire
Cutting tool
Ice pick
Needle and thread
Scissors
Black felt-tip marker

Procedure:

Cut the top section of the plastic container to four inches from the bottom. If you don't have another bottom section left over from some other project, you will need to cut one. Cut this to a depth of one and a half inches. Save all excess plastic. It can be used in many ways.

Cut two circles of felt four inches wide. Cut a strip of felt three inches long and half an inch wide. (The strip is for the handle.)

Make a pincushion for the top of the basket from the two circles of felt. Before you stitch these, punch holes around the top of the lid. Make these holes about half an inch apart in a circle three and a half inches wide.

Sew the three-inch strip together using an overcast stitch. Insert the wire through this strap of felt which has been stitched together.

Sew the felt circles together, leaving a small opening for stuffing. Put in cotton or other stuffing material. Complete the stitching around the felt circles. Punch two holes about half an inch apart through the felt circles. Insert the wire handle through the felt pincushion and on through the plastic basket lid.

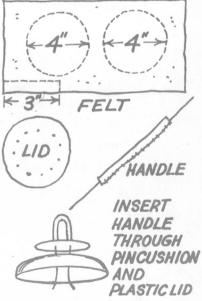

Twist the ends of the handle inside the basket lid to hold it in place. Lift the edges of the felt pincushion and put a little glue all the way around. Press the cushion down until it adheres to the basket top.

SEWING BASKET (Continued)

Turn the lid over, and sewing from the inside, stitch through the holes you made with the ice pick.

Glue a row of small rickrack around the top of the basket lid. Glue a row of larger rickrack around the lower edge of the lid and another row an inch from the bottom of the basket.

To make the basket smaller than the lid, so the lid will fit on easily, first clip two or three slits equidistant apart from the top of the basket down to an inch. Fold these slits over a quarter of an inch and staple in place.

Cut a circle of felt to fit the bottom of your basket and glue this in place. Make several small pockets of felt to hold such things as a thimble and measuring tape. Staple these in place along the top edge so they will hang inside the basket.

With a black felt-tip marker, you may wish to put on some saying such as, "A stitch in time saves nine."

TWIST WIRE HANDLE
INSIDE LID

CLIP AND FOLD OVER
. . . . STAPLE

12

WISHING WELL PLANTER

Materials:

One quart plastic bottle with cap
One yard of rickrack braid
Metal bottle cap about one inch high (for bucket)
Paint (two colors of enamel)
Paintbrush
Cutting tool (single-edged razor blade or knife)
Hammer and nail
Small lump of clay
A permanent plant
Glue

Procedure:

(a) Cut out a section on each side of the bottle about four inches wide and three inches long, leaving a one-inch shaft on each side. Begin cutting just below the bell-shaped portion.

Remove the cap from the bottle, and using a nail, make two holes in the cap about a quarter of an inch apart. Replace the cap.

Using enamel, paint the top section and the side shafts one color. Use a contrasting color for the bottom section.

(b) When this is dry, glue two rows of rickrack a quarter of an inch apart around the lower edge of the top section and one row near the top of the bottom section.

Make two holes with a nail on opposite sides of the bottle cap to be used as a bucket. Run a string through the holes in the cap at the top of the well and fasten to the holes in the sides of the bucket.

(c) Place a lump of clay in the bottom of the well and insert a permanent plant such as ivy.

CURLER CUP

Materials:

Half-gallon plastic bottle

Yarn (for hair)

Masking tape or other adhesive tape

Black and red felt-tip markers

Single-edged razor blade or other cutting tool

Stapler

Scissors

Procedure:

Cut the top section from the plastic bottle with a single-edged razor blade.

Draw on face features with felt-tip markers.

Staple six-inch loops of yarn from one side of face around to the other side. Staple two-inch loops across the front to form the bangs. Put the staples close together to hold the yarn hair in place. As you staple the yarn in place, let it extend to the inside of the container about half an inch.

Fasten the ends of the yarn down inside the container with tape.

CUT

DRAW ON FACE

STAPLE ON YARN HAIR

TAPE ENDS OF YARN DOWN INSIDE

PINCUSHION

Materials:

Quart plastic bottle

Five-inch circle of felt or other fabric

Cotton or other stuffing material

Small rickrack

Cutting tool

Glue

Stapler

Photograph

Procedure:

Cut top from bottle. Cut the remaining section in half vertically down to one inch from the bottom of the bottle. Cut across, separating the front half from the bottle. Round the corners of this piece, as well as the back half, so that they are the same shape.

Cut an opening in the section you cut away from the bottle. Make this a quarter of an inch smaller than the photograph. Glue the photograph to the back side. Place this section on top of the back section and staple around the edges. Glue rickrack to cover the staples.

Cut a five-inch circle of felt and stitch a quarter of an inch from the edge. Put cotton in the center and draw the thread up until your pincushion fits the bottom of the bottle. Glue this in place.

(To make a simpler project, use only the back half of the bottle with rounded corners. Tape the photograph in place with colored tape.)

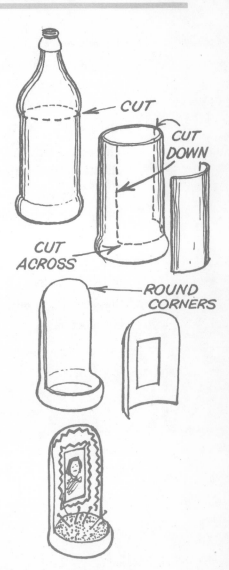

SPONGE AND SCRUB HOLDERS

Materials:

Two plastic bottles

Shears

Single-edged razor blade

Black and red felt-tip markers

Procedure:

To make the sponge holder, cut the top from a plastic bottle by using a single-edged razor blade.

Using the felt-tip markers, draw on the hair, the face features and a bow tie.

The scrub holder is made by first cutting the top from a plastic bottle by using a single-edged razor blade.

With shears, cut the front half away, leaving a cup at the bottom an inch in depth.

Cut a head shape from the back portion.

Draw in the face features and the hair with black and red felt-tip markers.

Make a design with the black marker around the top of the cup portion.

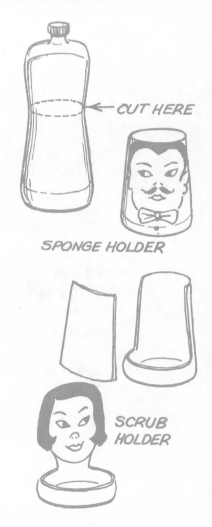

← CUT HERE

SPONGE HOLDER

SCRUB HOLDER

WASTEBASKET

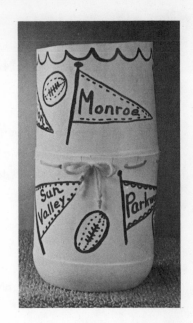

Materials:

Two gallon-sized plastic containers

Paper punch

Cutting tool

Large cord or yarn

Felt-tip marker

Procedure:

Cut the top from one container.

Cut the top and bottom from the second container.

Punch holes around the top of the first container an inch apart. Punch identical holes around the bottom of the second container.

Cut half-inch slits around the bottom of the second container about an inch apart.

Put the second container on the top of the first one so that the holes match. Using a bobbie pin or small safety pin, lace the two containers together with a large cord or yarn. (A shoestring can also be used for lacing.)

Put designs on with a felt-tip marker.

17

CLOWN BANK

Materials:

One-quart plastic bottle

Felt (red, black, white)

Fabric in gay color (dotted or striped)

Pinking shears

Cardboard

2½-inch styrofoam ball

Needle and thread

Single-edged razor blade

Procedure:

Cut collar and section to cover lower part of the bottle from the fabric. Cut hat, arms, bows, mouth, and nose from red felt. Cut eyes and brows from black felt.

Cut ears and shoes from cardboard.

Glue dotted material to lower part of bottle. Glue bows to shoes.

Glue the styrofoam ball to the neck of the bottle for the head. Glue hands to arms. Glue arms to the top of the bottle.

Slit the back of the collar, then place it around the neck of the bottle and glue together in the back.

Glue the face features in place. Insert the ears into the styrofoam ball. (Put a little glue on the ears before inserting them.)

Glue shoes to the bottom of the bottle.

Glue the bow tie at the neck.

Make the cap from felt and glue on the head.

Using a razor blade, cut a slot in the back for coins.

GLUE ARMS

LARGE BIRD CAGE

Materials:

One-gallon plastic bottle or jug

Two six-inch circles of styrofoam

Rickrack trim (37 inches)

Permanent flowers

Bird

Scissors

Single-edged razor blade

Glue

Procedure:

(a) Using a razor blade, cut the top and the bottom from the plastic jug.

(b) Cut the remaining cylinder in half vertically.

(c) Cutting horizontally, cut nine half-inch strips from each piece. Cut points on the ends of the strips.

(d) Put some glue on the ends and insert into the styrofoam circles. Leave about three fourths of an inch between each strip. Before completing the cage, insert some permanent flowers inside. Wire a bird on one of the flowers.

Insert the remaining strips to complete the cage. There should be 16 or 17 strips. Use the remaining strip to make a loop at the top of the cage for hanging.

Glue a row of rickrack trim around each of the styrofoam circles.

Your bird cage will be more colorful if you use colored styrofoam. Some supply houses carry these circles in a variety of colors.

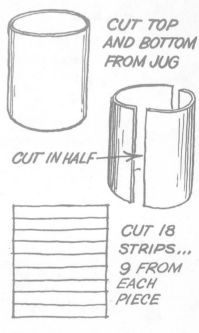

CUT TOP AND BOTTOM FROM JUG

CUT IN HALF

CUT 18 STRIPS... 9 FROM EACH PIECE

BEFORE COMPLETING CAGE INSERT FLOWERS AND BIRD

PIG BANK

Materials:

Half-gallon plastic bottle
Four large corks for legs
Red felt
One yard of red rickrack
Red chenille stick or a pipe cleaner
Felt-tip markers in black and green
Glue
Scissors
Single-edged razor blade
Red enamel
Small paintbrush
Ice pick

Procedure:

Cut eight large flowers from red felt. Cut the pig's ears and mouth from red felt. Glue the flowers onto the bottle. Space them so that they will cover any lettering that is on the bottle.

Using a razor blade, cut a slit on each side of the head for the ears. Put some glue on the lower edge of each ear and insert them in the slits. A knife blade will be useful in helping insert the ears. Glue the mouth in place.

Glue one row of rickrack in front of the ears and another at the back of the pig's body.

Using a black marker, make the pig's eyes. Make the leaves of the flowers with a green felt-tip marker.

Curl the chenille stick on your finger to make the tail. Make a hole in the back of the body with the ice pick. Put some glue on the end of the tail and insert it in the hole.

Glue the cork legs in place.

Paint the bottle cap red, using red enamel. When this is dry, screw tightly on the bottle to make the pig's nose.

Using the razor blade, cut a slot in the back for depositing coins.

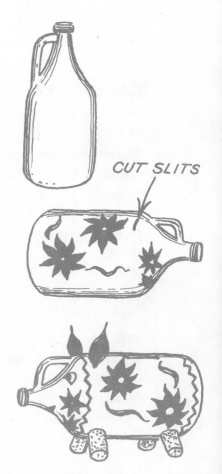

CUT SLITS

DOLLY DOORSTOP

Materials:

One-quart plastic bottle
Two-inch styrofoam ball
Two white plastic spoons
Fabric
Felt (black and red)
Yarn (for hair)
Two small bone rings
Pinking shears
Glue
Needle and thread
White adhesive tape
Pliers
Single-edged razor blade

Procedure:

Place plastic spoons in very hot water, and using pliers, bend them into a curved-arm shape.

Cut one-inch slits with the razor blade in the sides of the bottle near the top. These slits are for the arms.

Insert the arms and tape in place.

Fill the bottle with gravel, sand or other material to give it weight.

Cut a small slice from the bottom of the styrofoam ball to fit the bottle cap. Glue this in place.

Using pinking shears, cut the apron, collar and kerchief from fabric. Cut the buttons, face features and apron belt from felt.

Glue the felt belt to the apron. Glue the top of the apron to the bottle, letting the ends of the apron extend to the back.

Slit the collar open in the back. Place this on the bottle neck and glue the collar together in the back.

Screw the bottle cap in place so that you will know where to place the face features. Glue the face features in place. Glue the felt buttons down the center front.

To sew on the kerchief, place the styrofoam head in the center of the fabric triangle. Bring the lower corners up and sew together with the back point of the triangle.

Make loops of yarn over your finger for the hair. Sew this in the center front of the kerchief. Sew a bone ring on each side of the kerchief for earrings. Beads or buttons could be used for earrings.

CUT SLITS

TOOTHBRUSH HOLDER

Materials:

Quart-sized plastic bottle

Felt-tip markers in red and black

Felt for collar and buttons

Gingham or other fabric

Glue

Scissors

Procedure:

Cut the top from the bottle. Cut a slit down the center front to an inch from the bottom.

Cut from the slit around on each side two thirds up from the bottom, cutting an extension on each side to form arms.

Cut on up to form the head from the back portion of the bottle.

Cut a piece of fabric to fit the inside of the bottle doll. Cut two pieces to fit the arms. Glue the arm pieces on the outside and the body piece on the inside.

Cut collar, buttons and band from felt and glue in place. The band should be glued along the bottom edge of the base. Make the face, cap and name with felt-tip markers.

Staple the hands together to form holders for two toothbrushes.

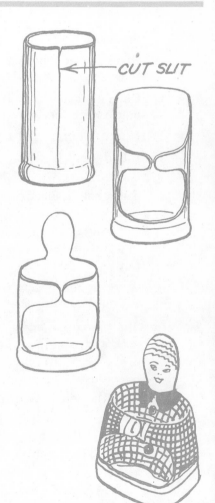

INDOOR BIRDHOUSE

Materials:

Quart plastic bottle

Felt (any color)

Net

Permanent flowers

Bird

Glue

Nail and hammer

Paper plate

Single-edged razor blade

Needle and thread

Using a razor blade, cut an opening for the door in the lower part of the bottle.

Cut a piece of felt to fit around the bottle. Cut an opening in this felt piece to fit the opening in the plastic bottle. Sew the felt together around the bottle.

Cut two strips of felt about half an inch wide. Sew one around the bottle cap and sew the other about two inches below this. To the lower band tack a permanent flower. Sew several more flowers on the lower part of the birdhouse, which is covered with felt.

Gather a piece of net and sew it around the upper portion of the birdhouse.

Glue a small paper plate to the bottom of the house. Glue or sew the bird's feet to the plate.

Using a nail, make two holes in the bottle cap. Insert a small wire or pipe cleaner to make a loop for hanging.

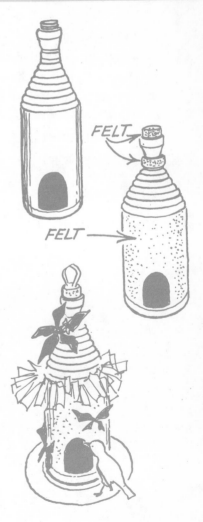

DISPLAY STAND

(To use for displaying items such as nature materials, dolls, etc.)

Materials:

Half-gallon plastic bottle

Black felt-tip marker

Single-edged razor blade

Scissors

Procedure:

Using the razor blade, cut the top from the bottle. Leave an inch and a half at the bottom as you cut away the front half. Round the corners at the top with scissors.

Using a felt-tip marker, put in all the lettering desired. This can be done on the inside back of the display stand or at the bottom outside part.

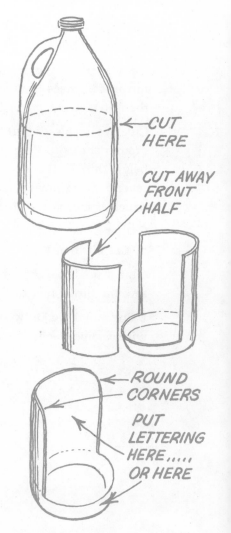

CUT HERE

CUT AWAY FRONT HALF

ROUND CORNERS

PUT LETTERING HERE..... OR HERE

FLOWER CAGE MOBILE

Materials:

Four 2½-inch circles of green styrofoam

Half-gallon plastic container

Cutting tool

Ruler

Pencil

Glue

Permanent flowers of vine type

Wire

Procedure:

Cut off top and bottom section of plastic container.

Cut in half vertically. Cut into strips half an inch wide. Cut eight strips for each cage. The ends of each strip should be cut to a point for inserting into the styrofoam. Cut one extra strip to make a loop for hanging, which should be about four inches long.

Put glue on ends of four-inch strip and insert into top of one styrofoam circle. Build the cage by inserting four strips of plastic equidistant apart from top piece of styrofoam to bottom piece. To help hold the strips in place, put a little glue on each end before inserting.

Insert a piece of wire in lower circle which will later be used to attach the second cage. This wire should be eight inches long.

Stick stems of flowers into lower styrofoam circle. Add other four plastic strips about half an inch apart until the cage is complete.

Make a second cage and join to first cage by the extending wire. Add a few leaves to the top of the second cage.

Cage mobile may be hung from the ceiling by using a small wire, or it may be hung on a wall bracket.

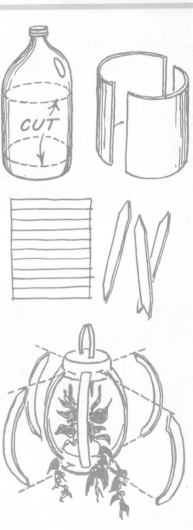

RABBIT EGG OR CANDY HOLDER

Materials:

One-quart plastic bottle
Red and black felt-tip markers
Knife
Scissors
Pencil

Procedure:

Cut the top from the bottle with a knife.

Cut the head shape and ears with scissors.

Using the felt-tip markers, fill in face features which have been sketched with a pencil. Make the nose pink by rubbing lightly with the red marker. The inner ears can be made pink in the same way or they may be colored red. Color the tie red. Make the other features with the black marker.

Partly fill the rabbit head with grass and add one or two colored eggs or candy.

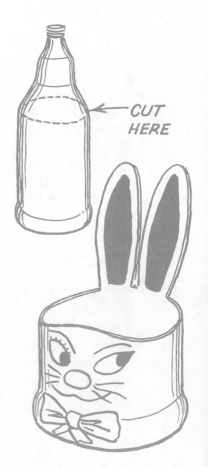

CUT HERE

FISH PLAQUE

Materials:

One-gallon plastic container or two
    half-gallon containers

Two or three large pine cones (the kind that
    are seven or eight inches long)

Piece of thin wood which is 18 inches long
    and 12 inches wide

Knife

Scissors

Glue

Black and green felt-tip markers

Pencil

Procedure:

Cut the top and bottom from a gallon plastic container with a knife. Using scissors, cut the plastic cylinder open.

Press the plastic sheet between paper with a warm iron to make it lie flat.

Make a paper pattern for the fish and grass stalks. The fish will need to be between seven and eight inches long. Trace the fish and grass stalks on the plastic and cut these out with scissors.

With a pencil, trace the plastic fish on the piece of wood in the position you want them to be.

Put on some old gloves and tear the sections from the pine cones.

Glue on some of the smaller sections of the cones to the fish you have traced on the wood for their fins. There will be four sections on top and two for the bottom fins.

Color the grass stalks with a felt-tip marker or enamels. Fill in the fish scales and other markings with a black felt-tip marker.

Glue fish and grass in place. It will help to weigh these down with rock or other heavy objects while they glue.

When the fish have been glued in place, glue two rows of pine cone sections across the end of the tail of each fish.

The frame of the plaque is made by overlapping sections of the pine cone all the way around the edge of the wood. Each section is glued in place before another is added. It will take between forty and fifty sections for the frame, depending on the size of the pine cone. Most of these sections from the large cones are an inch or more long.

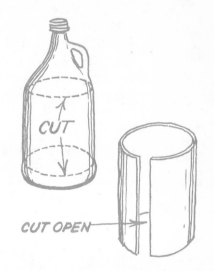

CUT OPEN

*GLUE PINE CONE
FINS IN PLACE*

FLOWER ARRANGEMENT

Materials:

One bottom section from a gallon plastic container

One bottom section from a half-gallon plastic container

Piece of green styrofoam seven inches long and two inches wide

Two small pieces of styrofoam (one piece one inch square and another piece large enough for your figurine to set on)

Two flat-headed nails two inches long

Cutting tool   Glue

Small wire   Permanent flowers

Spool   Green felt-tip marker

Pencil   Hammer

Procedure:

This is a project for using leftover bottom sections of the plastic containers. If you don't have these on hand, you could cut some. These bottom sections should be two inches deep. Punch a hole in the center of each plastic section. This can be done by placing the dish-type plastic over a wooden block and driving a nail through it.

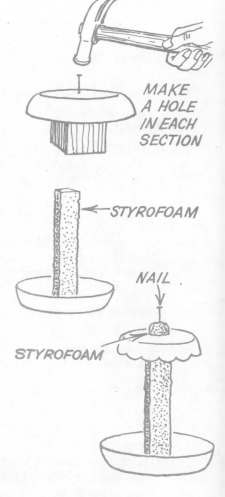

MAKE A HOLE IN EACH SECTION

Insert the nail in the lower section, which is the largest. Center the seven-inch piece of styrofoam on the point of the nail and push down until it stands upright. If the nail does not hold the styrofoam in place, put some glue under it on each side.

STYROFOAM

Using a spool, mark scallops around the edges of the smaller plastic section. Cut the scallops with scissors. Outline these with your green felt-tip marker. Enamels may also be used for the trim.

NAIL

Place the plastic section on top of the seven-inch styrofoam. Hold the one-inch piece of styrofoam on top of this just over the nail hole. Insert the nail through the one-inch styrofoam, the plastic section, and on into the upright styrofoam block. Wire vine-type flowers to the styrofoam center column. Insert small flowers in the one-inch piece of styrofoam on top.

STYROFOAM

Add a figurine to one side of the lower dish-type section. If you use a sitting figurine, add a small block of styrofoam as a seat. This can be glued in place.

DONKEY CADDY

Materials:

Pint plastic bottle (the kind that has a bell-shaped top)
Two wire coat hangers
Felt remnants
Ice pick
Enamel
Knife
Scissors
Needle and thread
Wire clippers
Tape
Cardboard (small piece)

Procedure:

Cut two inches from the top of the bottle. (This will be used for the head.) Cut five inches from the bottom of the bottle to be used for the body.

Cut the two wire hangers just above the straight portion at the bottom.

Bend the two pieces of wire as shown in the diagram. One piece will be used as the back legs and tail and the other as the front legs and neck.

Punch two holes at the front of the body two inches apart and about a quarter of an inch from the edge. Let the ice pick extend through the body, making two more holes just below the two on top. With the ice pick, punch two more holes a quarter of an inch from the back, and two just below these on the underside.

Punch two holes in the head—one in the center a quarter of an inch from the back edge, and another one just below it on the underside.

To join the front leg wire to the head, insert the wire through the lower hole and on through the upper hole. Bend the end of this wire down to the neck and tape the two wires together tightly.

Cut a round piece of cardboard to fit the front of the body. After this has been cut out, glue it in place.

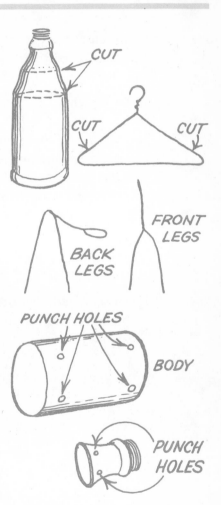

DONKEY CADDY *(Continued)*

Cut a piece from felt to fit over the open back part of the head and make the ears. Glue this felt piece to the back of the head.

Cut a straight piece of felt the length of the neck. This should be two inches wide. Fringe both sides of this piece by cutting to a depth of half an inch about an eighth of an inch apart. Put some glue in the center and on the sides of this piece and fold together over the taped wire to make the donkey's mane. Insert the front and back legs through the holes in the body. Bend the ends of the wire for feet.

The eyes may be painted or made with a felt-tip marker. The bottle cap can be painted with enamel if there is lettering on it.

Make the saddle bags of felt and trim them with rickrack or other decoration. Glue the center of the saddle bags to the donkey's back.

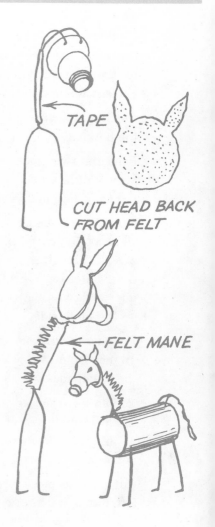

TAPE

CUT HEAD BACK FROM FELT

FELT MANE

BELT

Materials:

Half-gallon plastic container
Pair of shoestrings (about 36 inches, depending on waist size)
Paper punch (heavy-duty will work best)
Colored felt
Glue
Knife
Shears

Procedure:

To get the proper length of shoestrings, measure your waist and add twelve inches. The extra length is for tying.

Cut the top and bottom from the plastic container. Split the remaining plastic cylinder open.

Cut rectangular blocks from the plastic, which should be two inches long and an inch and a half wide. Cut these crossways from the plastic sheet so each block will be slightly curved. Cut 12 or 14 blocks, depending on waist size.

Punch a hole in the corner of each block an eighth of an inch from the edge.

Cut designs from felt and glue to the blocks. You might choose such designs as hearts, flowers, clover leaves, etc.

Lace the blocks together with the two shoestrings. Leave about six inches at each end of the belt for tying.

The belt may be worn with the tie in the front or back.

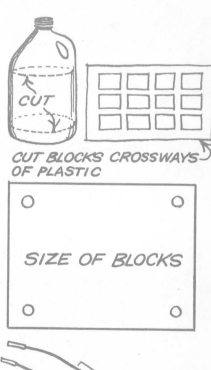

CUT BLOCKS CROSSWAYS OF PLASTIC

SIZE OF BLOCKS

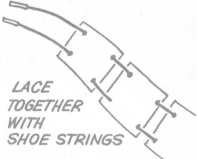

LACE TOGETHER WITH SHOE STRINGS

31

BASKET

Materials:

Gallon plastic container
Red or other colorful felt
Rickrack to match the felt
Green felt-tip marker or enamel
Glue
Cutting tool
Stapler
Paper
Pencil

Procedure:

Cut plastic container to a height of four or five inches.

Cut an inch and a half strip from the remaining upper section. Slit this open and staple an end to each side of the basket.

Glue a row of rickrack around the basket top and another row an inch from the bottom.

Cut a flower pattern from paper. Place this on your felt and draw four or five flowers. If your felt is dark, chalk could be used for tracing the flowers on the felt. After cutting the flowers out, glue them equally spaced around your basket.

Fill in the leaves with a green felt-tip marker.

Using this same idea, baskets can be made from any size plastic container.

By adding grass and colored eggs, these make attractive Easter baskets. They are also useful to hold fruit to carry to someone who is ill.

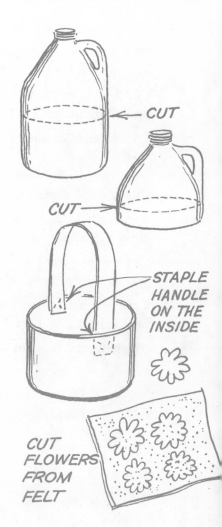

CUT

CUT

STAPLE HANDLE ON THE INSIDE

CUT FLOWERS FROM FELT

RABBIT NOTE PAD AND PENCIL HOLDER

Materials:

Red and black felt-tip markers
Knife
Shears
Stapler
Paper punch or ice pick
Paper
Pencil
Small note pad and pencil

Procedure:

Cut the top and bottom from the container. This can be done with a knife. Using shears, cut the remaining plastic cylinder open.

Using a warm iron, press this sheet of plastic between paper until it will lie flat. Caution—do not use a hot iron or your plastic may melt.

Make a rabbit-head pattern from paper as large as your plastic sheet will allow. Cut an additional pattern for the front portion which should be a quarter of an inch larger at the top than the back part so that when they are joined together the pocket holder will stand open slightly.

Mark around the pattern on the plastic with a pencil.

Cut the two pieces out with shears. Fill in the face features with a felt-tip marker. The nose and inner ears may be made pink by marking lightly with a red felt-tip marker.

Staple together around the edges. Punch a hole in the center top of the head with a paper punch or ice pick.

Insert a small note pad and a pencil.

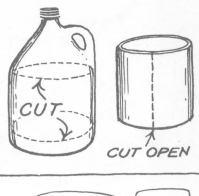

CUT OPEN

TRACE PATTERN ON PLASTIC

NAPKIN HOLDER
AND CLOWN TOOTHPICK HOLDER

Materials:

One-quart plastic bottle
Felt-tip markers or colored enamels
One two-inch styrofoam ball
Glue
Small red button or artificial holly berry
Black tape
Cutting tool

Procedure:

CLOWN TOOTHPICK HOLDER

Cut off all but the top two and a half inches of a plastic bottle. Cut a strip below this wide enough for the ears or about one and a quarter inches. Glue the styrofoam ball to the neck of the bottle. Cut the ears from the plastic strip—apply glue to the inner edge and insert into the styrofoam head.

Glue button or berry nose in place, and using a felt-tip marker or brush and enamels, make face features. Fill in other parts such as markings on ears, collar, etc. Add some black tape at the base of your clown. Let the tape fold to the inside to give a smooth edge. Add toothpicks to the top of the head, spacing them about a quarter of an inch apart.

NAPKIN HOLDER

From the lower section of the plastic bottle cut a vertical strip down each side an inch and a half wide. Cut this to within an inch from the bottom of the bottle.

Round corners of each side and decorate with colored felt markers or enamels.

BASE OF TOOTHPICK HOLDER
STRIP FOR EARS
NAPKIN HOLDER
CUT IN THREE SECTIONS

MASK

Materials:

Gallon plastic container
Black and red felt-tip markers
Elastic band
Paper punch or ice pick
Tape
Shears
Single-edged razor blade or other cutting tool

Procedure:

Cut the top from the container. Cut the lower section in half vertically. If the bottom of the container is too tough to cut with shears or a knife, try a small coping saw.

If your mask does not require ears, you can make two from one container. Since the rabbit mask in the photograph does have ears, these are to be cut from one side of the container. To make the face, round the lower edge of one half the plastic container with shears. Cut out the eyes and nose with a single-edged razor blade. Cut slits in the top for ears.

Put markings on the ears. The inside of the ear can be made pink by marking lightly with a red felt-tip marker. Insert the ears and tape them in place on the underside.

Complete the face features with the felt-tip markers. Punch a hole on each side of the mask and attach an elastic band. Many different masks can be made by using different face features.

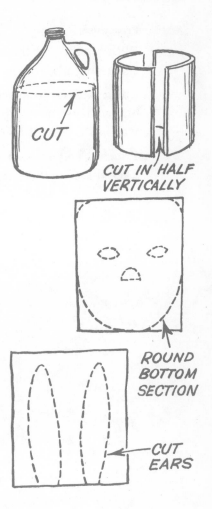

CUT

CUT IN HALF
VERTICALLY

ROUND
BOTTOM
SECTION

CUT
EARS

HEADBAND

Materials:

Pint plastic bottle
Paper punch
Colored shoestring (24 or 26 inches long)
Shears
Knife
Pencil

Procedure:

With a knife, cut the top and bottom off the bottle. Split the remaining plastic cylinder open.

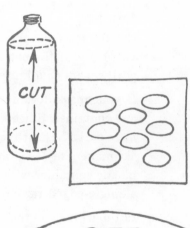

Cut a pattern from paper or cardboard and mark ovals or other shapes on the plastic with a pencil. Cut these crossways so each will be curved slightly.

Punch a hole in each end of the ovals with a paper punch. Lace these together with a colored shoestring.

Other designs may be used in place of the ovals, such as circles, squares or hearts. These could be decorated with small felt flowers.

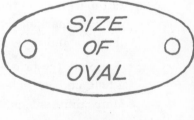

SIZE
OF
OVAL

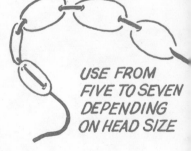

USE FROM
FIVE TO SEVEN
DEPENDING
ON HEAD SIZE

BELLS

Materials:

Top from a quart plastic bottle for each bell
Glass ball tree ornament
Small wire or chenille sticks
Aluminum foil
Rickrack (red is best)
Glue
Cutting tool
Red ribbon
Greenery
Nail
Hammer

Procedure:

This is a good project to use bottle tops left from other projects in which you did not use the tops. However, if you don't have the bottle tops, cut the top bell-shaped portion from quart-sized bottles.

Remove caps and punch a hole in the center of each. Replace caps and cover the entire plastic bell with aluminum foil.

Glue a row of red rickrack around the lower edge of each bell.

Thread a small glass ball on a piece of wire about seven inches long. Put a loop in the wire four inches from the glass ball to keep it in place after it is inserted in the bell.

Insert wire in the bell through the hole in the cap and make a loop at the top.

Tie several bells together and add some greenery. Tie a red ribbon at the top of the bell arrangement.

CUT HERE

TIE A LOOP IN WIRE

DOG BOOKENDS

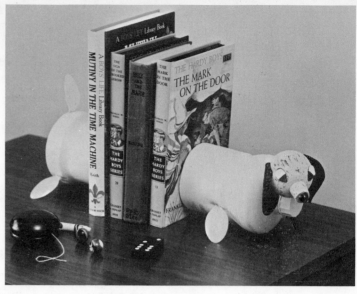

Materials:

One quart-sized plastic bottle

Five wooden spoons (do not use plastic as they may break)

Round cork (two or three-inch size)

Black felt (for ears)

Small cork (for nose)

Black button or bead

Plaster of Paris

Small wire or pipe cleaner

Waterproof tape

Scissors

Cut plastic bottle in half. Cut small slits for spoon feet and tail

Procedure:

After inserting the spoons for the feet and tail, put strips of tape on the outside of the bottle where you joined the legs to the body. This tape is to be removed later when the plaster hardens.

Cut ears and eyes from black felt. Glue a small piece of white paper on each eye to make the pupils. Glue the ears and eyes on the large round cork which will be the head. Glue a button on the end of the cork nose. After you glue the nose in place, insert a wire in the back of the head. This wire should be about five inches long.

Make a loop in the end of the wire to fit the neck of the bottle. Put the loop on the neck and screw the cap on tightly so that the head will stay in place.

Mix plaster with water until it is the consistency of whipped cream. Stand the half of the bottle which has the head in a can or other container to hold it upright. Stand the other part of the bottle upright. Pour plaster in each part of the bottle until well filled. If any plaster runs out around the legs, scrape it off before it begins to harden.

When the plaster hardens, glue circles of felt over the ends of the dog bookends.

CUT

MAKE UP A LOOP OF WIRE

GLUE ON FELT

LETTER HOLDER

Materials:

Quart plastic bottle (the type that is flat in front and back is best)
Red and green felt
Rickrack trim
Scissors
Knife
Glue

Procedure:

Using a knife, cut the top section from the bottle.

Cut down the sides of the bottle to three fourths of an inch from the bottom. Cut out a section on each side.

Round the back portion of the holder. Trim the front half an inch shorter than the back and round the edges.

Glue rickrack braid around the front section. Cut flowers and leaves from felt and glue onto the front of the letter holder. Glue a circle of felt in the center of the flower.

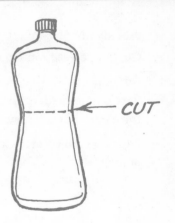

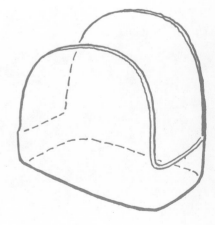

CANDLEHOLDER

Materials:

Half-gallon plastic bottle (the type that has a handle)

Felt (green and two other colors)

Rickrack trim

Glue

Scissors

Procedure:

Cut the top section from the bottle.

Cut flowers and leaves from felt. Glue these to the upper part of the holder. Glue a small circle of contrasting felt in the center of each flower.

Glue two rows of rickrack around the bottom part of the holder.

OLIVE AND CHEESE HOLDER

Materials:

Quart or pint plastic bottle
Large cork
Four popsicle sticks
Black felt
Black button
Round toothpicks
Glue
Ice pick
Knife
Pipe cleaner

Procedure:

Using a knife, carve the cork into a head shape.

Make four slits with the knife blade in the lower part of the bottle for the legs. Insert the popsicle sticks for legs.

Punch holes in the back with an ice pick for the toothpicks. Make these holes about an inch apart.

Cut a piece of felt to fit the cap of the bottle and glue this in place. (It would be best if you used felt the color of the bottle, if you have it.)

Glue the ears which you cut from felt to the cork head. Cut the tail from felt and glue it in place.

Fold a pipe cleaner in half. Twist the ends of the cleaner, leaving the center in loop form. Punch a hole with an ice pick on the underside of the head. Insert the ends of the pipe cleaner into this hole in the cork. Remove the bottle cap and place the loop end of the cleaner on the neck of the bottle. Screw on the cap to hold the head in place.

Glue the button onto the end of the nose. If the button has a shank, you will need to make an indention with the knife to fit this before gluing. Glue the felt eyes in place.

Insert round toothpicks in the back of the holder for olives and cheese.

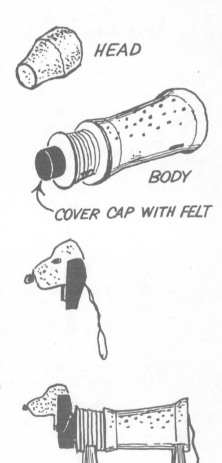

HEAD

BODY

COVER CAP WITH FELT

BIRD FEEDER

Materials:

Quart plastic bottle
Bottom section of two gallon plastic jugs
Wire coat hanger
Wooden spool
Ice pick
Single-edged razor blade
Enamel (any color)
Paintbrush

Procedure:

Cut the bottom from the two plastic jugs. Cut one so that it will be an inch and a half deeper than the other one.

Cut the top from a quart bottle.

Using an ice pick, punch a hole in the center of the two sections you cut from the plastic jugs.

Cut several openings in the bottom of the quart bottle. (This will allow the birdseed to feed into the lower section of the feeder.)

Cut the lower section from the coat hanger. Insert the wire into the top, which should be the deeper section you cut from a jug. Let the wire extend down through the quart bottle on through a wooden spool and finally through the other bottom section of the second plastic jug.

Bend the ends of the wire into a loop at the bottom of the feeder.

Fill the quart bottle with birdseed. Bend the wire at the top into a loop.

Paint the lower part of the container and the trim on the upper part with any desired color of enamel.

(Remember, something useful can be made from the remainder of the gallon plastic jugs. Look through this book for ideas and use some of your own.)

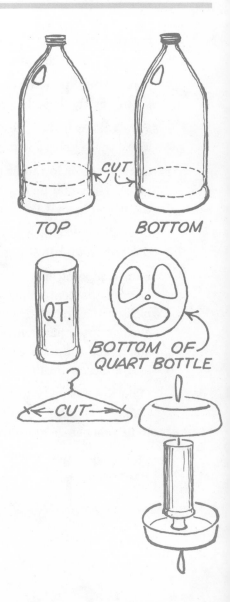

TOP   BOTTOM

QT.

BOTTOM OF
QUART BOTTLE

←CUT→

CANDY HOLDERS

Materials:

One quart-sized plastic bottle for each holder
Fabric or felt for the caps and collars
Black and red felt-tip markers
Glue
Scissors and a single-edged razor blade
Cotton (for Santa's beard and cap trim)
Needle and thread

Procedure:

Cut the top from the plastic bottle.

Cut the ears from white felt. Glue these in place. Draw face features and ear markings with a felt-tip marker.

Cut the cap from felt or other fabric to fit the top of the plastic bottle. Using an overcast stitch, sew around the cap. For the pixie, cut points around the cap and also around the collar.

For the Santa, glue cotton around the cap and at the tip of the cap. Glue some cotton on for the beard.

Bright red material should be used for the Santa and green for the pixie. Glue a row of rickrack trim around the base of the pixie. Glue a band of red felt around the base of the Santa.

COAT HANGER CLOWN

Materials:

Wire coat hanger
Old pair of stretchable hose
Felt (red, 7" x 20"—black, 3" x 12")
Silver glitter
Glue
Small wire
Scissors
Needle and thread

Procedure:

Bend the coat hanger in head form so that the top portion comes to a point and the lower part is rounded. Bend hook into loop.

From the bottom of the wire form slip on hose and pull to the top. Tie at top and bottom. Cut excess hose from wire form. Shape ears of wire and cover with portion of hose and sew in place. Ears can be made of felt if desired.

Cut face features, hat, collar and trimmings from felt. Working over a paper, glue these in place. Some glue may come through the hose and the paper will protect your working surface.

Make dots of glue on the hat, outline scallops on the collar, and tie center. Sprinkle with glitter. Shake excess glitter on a paper and return to the container.

Using the same wire and hose form, many different faces can be made. For school classes it would be less expensive to use construction paper in place of the felt.

A FEW OTHER FACE DESIGNS

Try working out some of your own.

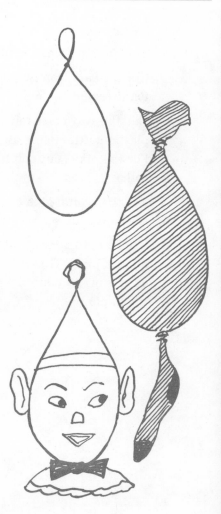

44

COAT HANGER FIGURES

Materials:

Coat hanger

Fabric

Felt

Small block of wood

Glue

Scissors

Wire clippers

Small drill

Enamel

Pencil

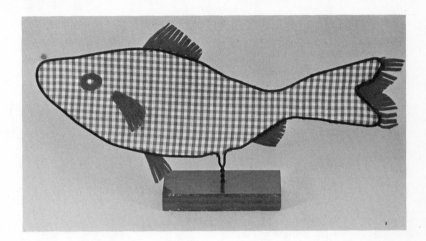

Procedure:

Pull wire into desired shape. Try to choose a simple figure such as a fish, at least for your first attempt to make a project of this kind. Using wire clippers, cut off the hook part of the hanger.

Place the wire figure on the fabric and draw around this with a pencil, leaving a margin of about an inch. Cut the design you have drawn from the fabric.

Put glue on one side of the wire frame of your figure. Place this on the fabric, making sure the fabric extends from the wire frame all the way around. Stretch the fabric until all the wrinkles are out. Allow the glue to adhere the fabric to the frame. Using small sharp scissors, trim the excess fabric from your figure.

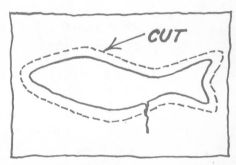

Add felt trimmings such as eyes and fins if you are making a fish. Drill a hole about three fourths of the way through the center of the block of wood. Paint the block which makes the base for your figure or design. When this is dry, insert the wire extended from your design in a position so that it will stand.

Many other designs can be made by using this same method, such as ducks, clown heads, snowmen, or any figure that is not too difficult to bend. You might choose some fabric that is the same as the curtains in your room or that blends well with the colors of your room. It is best to use a fabric that is not too thick.

BUTTERFLY

Materials:

Two wire coat hangers
Black felt (14" x 4")
Black sewing thread, needle
Two buttons (for eyes)
Three yellow chenille sticks or colored pipe cleaners
Pair of old stretch-type hose (seamless)
Cotton or other stuffing material
Glitter
Scissors
Glue
Wire clippers
Tape (adhesive)

Procedure:

Cut hooks from coat hangers, leaving a straight piece of wire two inches long below the hook portion. Bend the wire hangers in the shape of wings.

Slip a hose on each wing. Put the lower end of the wing in the open part of the hose and pull the top all the way to the top of the wing, then pull on down to the straight wire where the hook was cut off. Tie the hose just below the thick top portion to the wire. Pull the foot part of the hose until it is stretched tightly. Tie at the lower wing tip and clip excess hose here and also at the center wire. Make the second wing in the same way.

Cut body and wing spots from black felt. Tape the two wings together in the center.

Sew the body two thirds of the way up from the bottom and stuff. Place wings between the body parts and sew together, leaving a small opening for stuffing. Complete stuffing and sewing of head. Curl the ends of two chenille sticks and sew to end of head. Sew button eyes in place.

Glue wing spots in place. Outline stripes on body and lower half of wing spots with glue. Sprinkle with glitter. When this has adhered, shake excess glitter onto a paper and pour back into the container.

Bend a piece of chenille stick in loop form and sew to the back of your butterfly for hanging.

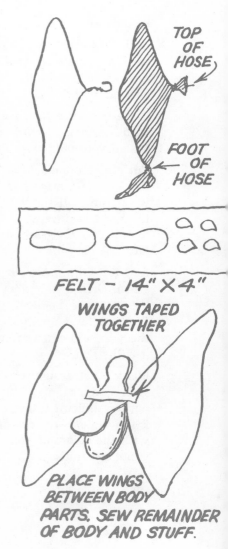

TOP OF HOSE

FOOT OF HOSE

FELT — 14" X 4"

WINGS TAPED TOGETHER

PLACE WINGS BETWEEN BODY PARTS. SEW REMAINDER OF BODY AND STUFF.

BOOK RACK

Materials:

Two wire coat hangers

Black adhesive tape

Felt remnants

Glue

Cardboard

Needle and thread

Scissors

Procedure:

Bend each of the two hangers in the following way: Start three inches from the center and bend the end of the hanger back, making a kind of arm that extends about five inches. Bend the ends of both hangers in this way.

Slip the bent ends together until there is a distance of five inches between the hook part of the two hangers. Tape the lower sides of the hangers together using black tape.

Bend hook into loop form. From felt make heads or other designs to fit over the loop part of the hangers. Make these double and sew on top and sides. Cut a piece of cardboard similar in form and insert in felt piece. This will help hold it in place when placed on wire loop. Cut face features or trimmings from felt and glue them in place.

After slipping designs on hangers, tack them with needle and thread at the bottom edge.

There are many designs you might use, such as animals, club emblems, people, etc.

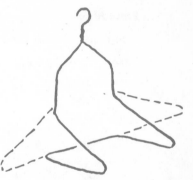

BEND ENDS OF HANGERS AS SHOWN

LEAVE ABOUT 5" BETWEEN HANGERS

5"

TAPE HERE

DUTCH DOLL TISSUE HOLDER

Materials:

One wire coat hanger
Half of a two-inch styrofoam ball
Piece of colored felt about 10" x 5"
Small amount of red, black, and white felt or paper for face
  features
Yarn (for hair)
Scissors
Glue
Rickrack trim
Straight pins
Needle and thread
Adhesive tape

Procedure:

Bend the hook of the hanger into a loop.

Place the hanger on the felt and draw around the upper portion to make a piece to be used for the waist. This piece will be about 10 inches long and 3 inches wide in the center. After cutting this out, cut a strip 7 inches long and 1½ inches wide.

Cut the ends of this strip to a point to make the hat.

Using an overcast stitch, sew the waist portion to the hanger. Make the hair by plaiting 10-inch strands of yarn which have been tied in the center. To make bangs, wrap yarn around your finger to form loops. Sew this to the center of the yarn hair and clip the loops to make straight bangs.

Tape the half of the styrofoam ball just below the loop of the hanger.

Pin on the doll's hair with straight pins.

Turn back the front of the strip you cut for the hat, and just back of this fold pin the hat in place. Glue a row of rickrack trim along the front edge.

Glue rickrack trim along the edges where you sewed the felt to the hanger. Glue a row of the braid down the center front of the waist. Glue the face features in place.

Bend the ends of the hanger to hold a box of tissues.

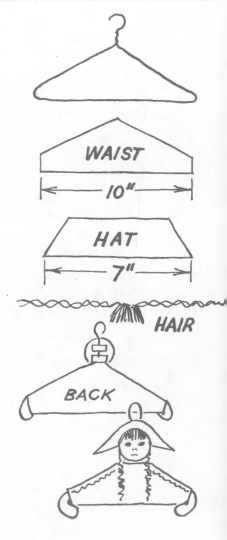

HEART HOSE HAMPER

Materials:

One wire coat hanger

Felt (12" x 20")

Three buttons

Rickrack

Thread

Needle

Scissors

Chalk

Glue

Pins

Procedure:

Bend the wire hanger into a heart shape. Bend the hook into a loop. Place the heart-shaped wire form on the felt and draw around it with chalk, allowing half an inch margin.

Use the wire form as a guide to cut the front piece. Trace the heart with chalk on the felt two thirds of the way up from the bottom. It is not necessary to leave a margin on the front piece as it can be pinned in place later.

Put glue on the back of the wire form. Place this on the felt heart you cut first. Be sure that the wire form touches the felt all the way around. When the felt has adhered to the wire, clip all excess felt from around the heart frame.

Glue two rows of rickrack across the top of the second piece of felt you cut. Sew three buttons down the center of this piece.

Pin the front piece in place, which will later become a pocket-type holder.

Using an overcast stitch, sew all the way around the felt heart.

Initials cut from felt or other decorations could be used in place of the buttons.

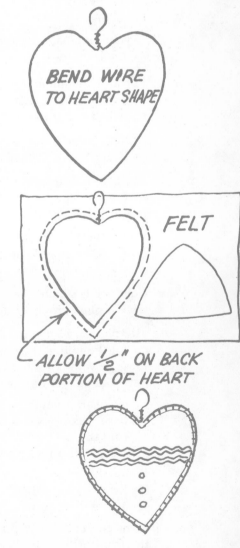

BEND WIRE TO HEART SHAPE

FELT

ALLOW ½" ON BACK PORTION OF HEART

CLUB EMBLEM PAPERWEIGHT AND PENCIL HOLDER

Materials:

One wire coat hanger
Green fabric (or your club colors)
White felt or lightweight cardboard
Plaster of Paris (about half a pound)
Photograph
Small cardboard box (such as a pill box)
Glue
Wire clippers
Chalk
Pencil
Scissors

Procedure:

If your club has a simple-shaped emblem, such as Girl Scouts or 4-H Club, this project will not be too difficult.

For a 4-H emblem, shape the wire hanger into a large four-leaf clover shape. Cut the hook from the hanger, leaving an extended wire of two and a half inches.

If your fabric is dark, use chalk after placing your wire form on it and mark around it, leaving half an inch margin.

Put glue on the back of the wire form and place on the four-leaf clover you have cut from the fabric. Pull the edges before it glues together so it will not be wrinkled.

When the fabric has adhered to the frame, clip all excess fabric from around the clover design with sharp small scissors.

Cut four H's from felt or cardboard and glue them in place. Glue a photograph in the center.

Mix plaster with water until it is the consistency of whipped cream. Pour this in a small cardboard box and allow to set for a few minutes. Insert clover design and hold in place until the plaster hardens enough to hold it upright.

To make an opening for the pencil, insert a pencil in the plaster base while it is still soft and turn it around several times, making the hole a little larger than the pencil. Remove the pencil and clean all plaster with a damp cloth.

When the plaster is hard, peel away the plaster from the cardboard box. Edges of plaster base may be sanded or scraped with a knife to make it smooth.

Print the club motto, if desired, on cardboard and glue to the front of the paperweight.

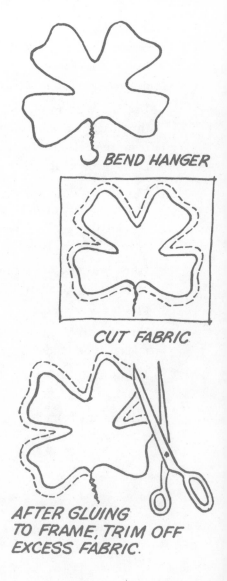

BEND HANGER

CUT FABRIC

AFTER GLUING
TO FRAME, TRIM OFF
EXCESS FABRIC.

COAT HANGER PICTURE FRAME

Materials:

Wire coat hanger
Cardboard
Picture
Glue
Needle and thread or yarn
Scissors

Procedure:

Shape hanger into loop form.

Place this on a cardboard and draw around it with a pencil. After cutting the cardboard, glue a colorful picture on, such as you might find on the cover of a magazine.

Put glue on the back of the wire loop and lay this on your picture which has been mounted on cardboard. Be sure the wire touches the cardboard all the way around. When this has adhered, you may trim off the excess cardboard if there is any.

Using a large needle and thread, make overcast stitches all the way around the picture.

Bend the hook of the hanger into a loop for hanging.

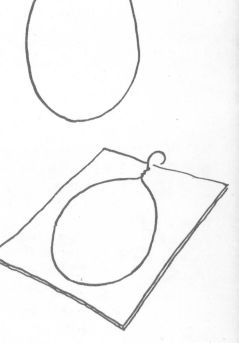

FRUIT

Materials:

Styrofoam balls
Old candles or other wax
Bits of wax crayons
Wire
Stem tape
Permanent leaves
Cloves
Wire clippers and a knife
Styrofoam block
Old tin cans or double boiler
Source of heat
Pins

Procedure:

By pressing styrofoam balls with your hands, shape them into desired shapes. Different size balls may be used for a variety of fruits. To make a pear, trim off the sides and bottom of one ball so it will fit on another. Join the two balls with pins.

Insert wire stems into styrofoam fruit, leaving a length of about five inches. Melt old candles over low heat, using a double boiler. Tin cans may be used by placing a medium can inside a larger can partially filled with water. Add bits of crayons until the desired color is obtained. Remove old candle wicks and stir well.

Remove from heat. When the wax will coat a spoon you may begin dipping your fruit. Holding the stem, dip fruit until it is well coated with wax. It may take several dippings to obtain an even coating.

As the dipping process is completed, insert the stem end of fruit in a piece of styrofoam for it to harden. To give a rough texture to such fruits as oranges and lemons, roll them on a food grater or screen wire while the wax is still soft. Some fruits, such as apples or plums, should be rubbed with the fingertips to give a smooth surface.

Insert a clove in the end of apples and pears.

Add leaves to the fruit and wrap the stems with green stem tape. This type of fruit is very light weight and may be easily wired to a flat basket for hanging. If you wish to use your fruit in a bowl, you will need to cut the stems to a short length.

PRESS STYROFOAM BALLS INTO FRUIT SHAPES

PIN PARTS OF PEAR TOGETHER

ADD WIRE

DIP FRUIT INTO MELTED WAX

PLACE ON STYROFOAM TO DRY

INSERT CLOVE INTO APPLES AND PEARS

ADD LEAVES

IMP PENCIL HOLDER

Materials:

Nine-inch cardboard tube

Six-inch styrofoam circle

Four red plastic spoons

Felt (white, red, and black)

Small piece of cardboard (5 inches square)

Tape (adhesive or freezer)

Scissors

Knife

Fabric

Procedure:

Cut the cardboard tube so that one section will be six inches long and another section will be three inches long. Put the end of the tube on a piece of cardboard and draw around it with a pencil. Make two circles and cut them out.

Put glue around the edges of the cardboard circles and glue to the bottom of the pieces of tube.

To make the legs, tape a plastic spoon to each side of the lower end of the six-inch piece of cardboard tube.

Cut a piece of fabric to cover each piece of the tube, allowing half an inch for hems. Fold up a quarter inch on the fabric cut for the longer piece of tube. Cover the tube with glue and wrap the fabric on.

Tape a spoon on each side of the upper part of the tube for arms.

Cut a piece of white felt two inches wide and long enough to go around the tube. Cut ears from the felt. Cover the top portion of the tube with glue.

Wrap the felt on the tube and hold it until it is glued in place. Glue the ears on. Cut the face features, collar and buttons from felt and glue these in place.

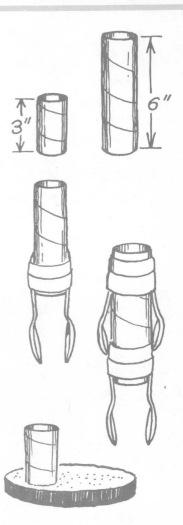

IMP PENCIL HOLDER   *(Continued)*

To make the holder for short pencils, use the three-inch piece of tube. Turn down a quarter inch at the top and bottom of the fabric. Cover the tube with glue and wrap the fabric on. Place this small container to one side of the styrofoam circle. Insert a large-headed pin inside to hold the container in place.

Cut a one-inch wire strip of felt long enough to go around the styrofoam circle. Glue the felt strip around the circle.

Insert the imp's plastic spoon feet into the styrofoam circle until it will stand upright.

Place long pencils in the imp and short ones in the small container.

TOOHPICK HOLDER

Materials:

Small glass bottle (2 ounce)
Two-inch styrofoam ball
Cardboard (for ears)
Felt (red, black and two contrasting colors)
Two blackeyed peas (for eyes)
Holly berry (permanent)
Flat type toothpicks
Glue
Black felt-tip marker
Needle and thread
Scissors

Procedure:

Cut a small slice from the styrofoam ball so that it will fit on the bottle cap. Glue this in place.

Cut the collars from contrasting colors of felt. The lower collar should be a quarter inch larger than the top collar.

Make the bow and buttons from the same color as the lower collar. Glue the buttons down the front of the bottle. Glue a strip of felt around the bottle cap.

Place the top collar on the lower one and sew the bow at the center top. Sew the collars together on the bottle at the back. Before making the face features be sure the cap is screwed on tightly. Cut the ears from the cardboard and put the marking on with a felt marker. Put a little glue on the point of the inner ear and insert into the head.

Cut face features from felt and glue in place. If you don't have a holly berry, a small circle of red felt may be used for the nose. Glue the berry nose in place. Put glue on the peas and press them in place for eyes.

Insert the smaller end of two or three dozen toothpicks in the top of the ball head. Store a supply of toothpicks in the bottle.

COLLARS

TIE

EARS

PILL BOTTLE

Materials:

Small glass bottle

Styrofoam ball (1½ inches or select according to size of bottle used)

Two blackeyed peas (for eyes)

Felt in red, black, and white

Permanent red holly berry (for nose)

White cardboard (for ears)

Glue

Scissors

Needle and thread

Small piece of fabric

Procedure:

Cut a small slice from the styrofoam ball to fit the top of the bottle cap. Glue the ball to the cap.

Cut arms, collar and mouth from red felt. Cut tie, hands and neckband from white felt. Glue hands to arms. Sew the arms to the collar. Sew the tie to the center of the collar. Sew the collar together at the back of the bottle.

Glue the felt buttons down the front of the bottle. Glue the neckband around the bottle cap.

Screw the cap on the bottle. Cut the ears from the cardboard and put on the markings with the felt-tip marker. Put a little glue on the point of each ear and insert into the styrofoam ball. Make hair and eyebrows with the marker. Put the glue on the peas and press them in place with your thumb. (You might add a little red nail polish to make the eyes appear bloodshot.) Glue the nose in place. You could use a small circle of felt in place of the berry for a nose.

Make a miniature ice bag from the fabric and tie it on the bottle doll's head with a small piece of gauze or other material.

EARS

CARDBOARD ANIMALS

Materials:

Cardboard tubing (such as waxed paper
   or foil is wrapped on)

Colored cardboard

Black felt-tip marker

Yarn

Glue

Pipe cleaner (for cat's tail)

Scissors

Single-edged razor blade

Procedure:

CAT

Using a razor blade, cut a piece of tubing three and a half
inches long. Cover this with glue, then wrap with yarn. Cut
the back and front of the cat from yellow cardboard. Make
the face features and stripes with a felt-tip marker or crayon.
Add a pipe cleaner to the back portion for the tail.

Glue the head and back portion to the yarn-covered tubing.

GIRAFFE

For the giraffe, follow the same procedure, except cut the
tubing four inches long.

Cut the long-necked giraffe from yellow cardboard. Cut a
front and back portion.

After wrapping the tubing with yarn, glue the front portion
and back part in place.

Make spots and face features with a black felt-tip marker.
Insert half a pipe cleaner for the tail.

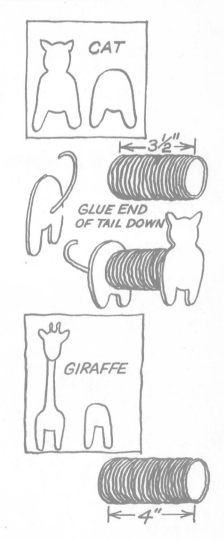

SHOE BOX CAT

Materials:

Shoe box
Cardboard
Yellow felt
Black felt-tip marker
Stapler
Scissors
Glue

Procedure:

Cut one set of legs, face and tail from cardboard. Cut another set from yellow felt.

Make stripes and face features on the felt with the black felt-tip marker.

Staple cardboard legs to lower part of the box.

Staple the tail and head to the lid of the box.

Cover the cardboard parts well with glue and place felt parts on these. Smooth out any wrinkles in the felt as you glue each piece on.

In selecting a box, try to get one with lettering only on one end.

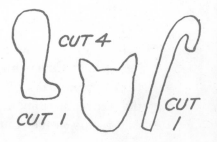

CHRISTMAS CARD HOLDER

Materials:

Red felt

Small amounts of green, white, and black felt

Cardboard (heavy)

Small cardboard box

Glue

Four brads

Scissors

Small red rickrack

Procedure:

Cut a boot from cardboard. It should be about 12 inches high and the foot should be 9 inches long. Using this as a pattern, cut another boot from felt, making it a quarter inch larger.

Try to select a box which can be cut to five inches in height. The depth of the box should be about 2 inches. The box width should be the same as the leg part of the boot so that it will fit well on it.

Cover the box with red felt on all sides except the back. This should be glued in place. Glue the red felt boot to the cardboard boot.

Punch a hole in the box corners and in the boot where they are to be joined. Insert a brad in each hole and spread the ends to hold the box in place.

Cut a piece of white felt two and a half inches wide and half an inch longer than the top of the boot. Glue this in place, then add a row of small red rickrack around the edges.

Cut letters for your name or "Merry Christmas" from black felt. Red felt could also be used for the lettering. Glue the letters in place.

From green felt, cut leaves and a stem for a sprig of holly. Cut a few red berries from red felt. Glue the holly on the front of the box. Glue a piece of red felt on the inside of the box to cover the brads.

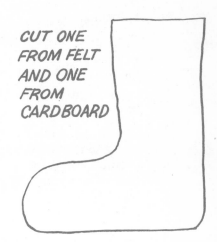

CUT ONE FROM FELT AND ONE FROM CARDBOARD

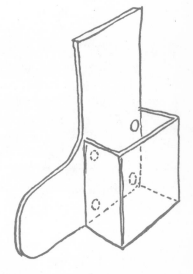

HUMPTY DUMPTY BOX

Materials:

Oatmeal box

White oilcloth or paper

Fabric

Felt (one piece colored and one piece white)

Rickrack trim

Yarn

Glue

Scissors

Felt-tip markers in red and in black

Procedure:

Cut a piece of oilcloth or white paper three and a half inches wide and long enough to fit around the box. Allow about half an inch for overlap.

Cut a piece of colorful fabric four inches wide and the length of the oilcloth.

For the arms, cut two pieces of felt three inches long and an inch and a half wide. Cut strips of felt seven inches long and one and a half inches wide for the legs. Cut a piece of felt half an inch wide and long enough to go around the box lid.

Cut the hands and feet from white felt or oilcloth.

Glue the white oilcloth on the top half of the box. Glue the fabric on the lower section, allowing it to overlap on the oilcloth. Glue the felt strip around the box lid. On top of this, glue a row of rickrack. Also glue a row of rickrack around the middle of the box.

Glue the feet and hands on to the strips of felt cut for the legs and arms.

Make the face features with the felt-tip markers.

Cut two slits for the legs at the bottom of the box near the front. Allow an inch between the legs. Cut two slits for the arms just above the fabric. These slits should be the width of the felt strips.

Push the felt arms and legs into the slits with a knife blade. On the inside of the box the ends should be glued down.

Make a pompon for the box lid by wrapping yarn around a three-inch piece of cardboard. Slip this off and tie in the center. Cut the loops and glue the pompon in the center of the box lid.

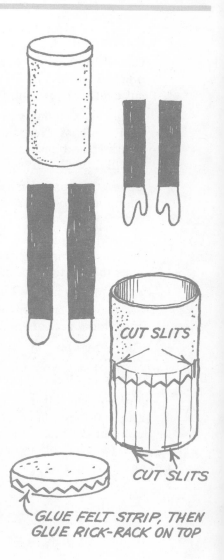

CUT SLITS

CUT SLITS

GLUE FELT STRIP, THEN
GLUE RICK-RACK ON TOP

CAT DOORSTOP

Materials:

One soft-drink bottle (without raised lettering)
Three-inch styrofoam ball
Black enamel
Paintbrush
Felt (black, red, and some contrasting color)
Two white buttons (for eyes)
One small rhinestone button (for nose)
Glue
Wire (12 inches)
Scissors
Black sewing thread and needle
Knife
Bottle filled with gravel or sand

Procedure:

With a knife, cut a hole in the styrofoam ball about as large as the mouth of the bottle. Put some glue in the hole, then insert the neck end of the bottle, pressing down on the styrofoam until it is glued in place.

Paint the bottle and the attached ball with black enamel. Paint the pupils on the button eyes.

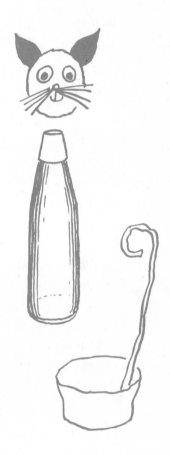

Cut a small tongue from red felt. Cut a circle of black felt an eighth of an inch larger than the bottom of the bottle. Cut another piece an inch and a half wide and long enough to fit around the circle you cut. Sew this strip around the circle. This makes a felt cup to fit the bottom of the bottle.

For the tail, cut a strip of black felt an inch wide and twelve inches long, tapering one end. Fold the felt tail in half and stitch. Insert the wire in the tail. Sew the tail to the inside of the felt cup you made for the bottom of the bottle. Curl the end of the tail. When the bottle is dry, set it in the felt cup.

Cut the ears and whiskers from black felt. Cut two slits in the ball where the ears are to be.

Put a little glue on the lower end of the ears and, using a knife, insert them in the head.

Put some glue on the eyes and press them in place. After gluing the tongue in place, glue the whiskers just above it. Glue the rhinestone button over the ends of the whiskers where they join the head to make the nose.

Make the collar about an inch and a half wide of any color of felt.

CLOWN AND DOG

Materials:

Piece of styrofoam approximately 10" x 14" and
   1 inch thick
Yarn (white and two other colors)
Red and black felt
Three buttons
Straight pins
Glue
Knife
Scissors
Needle and thread
Gold spray paint

Procedure:

Cut clown body and shoes from styrofoam.

Wrap the head and hands with white yarn. When you are to
the place to change colors, wrap the yarn several times and
sew the ends in place. Overlap the yarn used to make the
shirt and gradually extend downward and out to cover the
arms. To cover the styrofoam base, you will need to criss-
cross the yarn in front and back as you do your wrapping.
Sew the ends of the yarn at the waist.

Overlapping the ends of the yarn used for the waist, wrap a
contrasting color to cover the lower part to make the clown's
pants.

Cut the shoes from styrofoam. Spray with gold paint; pin
these in place.

Cut the cap, neckband, belt, shoe bows, ears and face features
from felt. Glue the face features on. Sew the belt and collar-
band on. Pin or sew the bows on the shoes. Make the cap
and sew on at the back of the head. Sew the ears in place.
Sew on the buttons down the waist front.

SHOES

BODY

TACK
ENDS
OF
YARN

PIN
SHOES

YARN COVERED DOG

Materials:

Styrofoam (about 4 inches square)
Five pipe cleaners
Yarn
Black felt
Needle and thread
Scissors
Knife

Procedure:

Cut the dog's body from styrofoam. Fold a pipe cleaner in the center so there will be a loop at the end for each leg. Insert these in place. Insert a pipe cleaner for the tail.

Wrap the entire dog with yarn, overlapping so all the styrofoam base will be covered. With a needle and thread, tack the yarn at the ends of the feet and tail to keep it from slipping off.

Cut eyes, ears and collar from felt. Glue the eyes in place. Sew on the ears and collar.

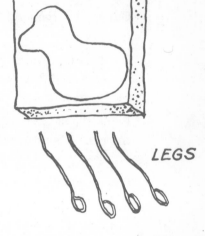

LEGS

TACK

63

DOOR SWAG
(Christmas Decoration)

Materials:

Three small aluminum pie pans
Red ribbon (14 inches long and 1 inch wide)
Red cardboard
Three small glass tree balls
Wire (6 inches long)
Small bone ring
Scissors
Stapler
Red thread
Needle
Ice pick

Procedure:

Cut the top section from each pan, leaving only the flat bottom section.

Cut slits all the way around the top section a quarter of an inch apart. Cut circles the size of the rim of the pans from red cardboard.

Bring the slits of foil to the inside and flatten them out on the rim of the pans. Staple these to the cardboard circles.

Cut a four-petal flower from the bottom of each pan. Curl the edge of each flower slightly.

Punch a hole in the center of each flower with an ice pick. Cut the wire into two-inch lengths. Put a two-inch wire through the metal loop of each glass ball.

Put the flowers in the centers of the cardboard circles. Insert the wire on the balls through the flowers and cardboard circles. Spread the wires on the back side to hold the balls and flowers in place.

Staple these on a red ribbon one inch apart. Sew a bone ring at the top for hanging. (If you don't have a bone ring, a loop of wire could be used.)

PAPERWEIGHT
AND PENCIL HOLDER

(Since the bulb is glass, this project is not recommended for children.)

Materials:

Plaster of Paris (about half a pound)
Burned-out light bulb (75 or 100-watt)
Small cardboard box (3″ x 4″)
Woman's old hose
Felt (black and red)
Needle and thread
Sandpaper
One color of enamel
Spoon and container for mixing plaster

Procedure:

Select a box such as a pill box or other small box. If the box is tall, cut it down to a height of about three inches.

Slip the bulb into the part of the hose just above the foot. Tie the hose at the base of the bulb and also at the top. Cut off foot portion near the base of the bulb.

Cut the top of the hose to a length of eight inches. Cut this into three equal strips and braid to half an inch from end, then tie with a sewing thread.

Cut face features from felt and glue in place.

The hat is made by cutting a two and a half inch circle from black felt and a strip eight inches long and one inch wide. Sew the strip together, then sew the circle to this, completing the hat.

Measure the base of the bulb and cut a piece of black felt long enough to go around it for the collar. This should be three fourths of an inch wide.

TIE

CUT TO A LENGTH OF 8″

2½″

8″ x 1″

POUR PLASTER INTO BOX

PAPERWEIGHT
AND PENCIL HOLDER   *(Continued)*

Mix plaster with water until the consistency of whipped cream. Pour into a cardboard box. When this begins to harden, insert bulb head into plaster and hold upright until it will stand erect. While plaster is still soft, insert a pencil at one side of the head and make a hole by turning the pencil from side to side a few times. Remove the pencil and clean with a cloth.

When the plaster has hardened, peel away the cardboard box. Sand the plaster base on the corners or any rough places.

Paint the base with a bright enamel, such as yellow or green. When this is dry, add the collar by sewing the lower edge together. Felt may be glued to the bottom of the paperweight if desired. Replace the pencil in the holder.

MACARONI TREE

Materials:

Ten-inch cardboard cone (type used in textile mills for thread)
Shell macaroni
Glue
Cardboard
Dessert dish
Gold spray paint

Procedure:

Cut a cardboard circle to fit over the end of the cone. Glue this in place.

Glue the cone to an inverted dessert dish. Spray well with gold paint.

Glue rows of shell macaroni around the cone until it is completely covered.

Spray the macaroni-covered cone tree with gold paint.

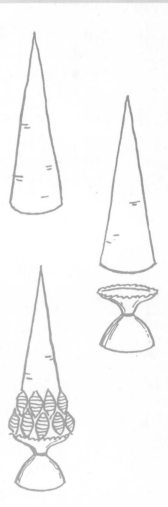

TV TRAY MASK

Materials:

TV tray for each mask
Colored construction paper
Pipe cleaners or small wire
Scissors
Glue
Tape
Black felt-tip marker or crayon

Procedure:

Punch two holes with tip of scissors in center of tray about half an inch apart. Insert cleaner or wire for hanger.

Cut face parts, horns, etc., from colored construction paper. Felt or other fabric may be used in place of the paper.

Glue face parts in place. From the back side of the tray, tape ears or horns in place. Complete face features with a felt-tip marker or crayon.

Many different kinds of masks may be created, using different colors and designs. Shown are a few you might try. Make up some characters of your own.

BACK of TRAY

BIRDS FROM OLD CANDLES

Materials:

Old candles

Styrofoam

Bits of wax crayons

Chenille sticks or small wire

Black and yellow enamels

Feathers

Cutting tool

Root or limb for mounting birds

Container

Spoon

Procedure:

Outline the body shape of bird on styrofoam block. Cut this out with a knife or other tool. Press the edges with your fingers to give a rounded effect, or carve them with a knife. For aid in dipping process, insert a wire ten inches long in area where legs will be. Bend wire together.

Melt wax in double boiler over low heat. Remove from heat and allow to cool until the wax will coat a spoon. Dip bird body in wax until it is well coated with wax. As the wax becomes firm, rub it gently with your fingertips to give a glossy surface.

Insert wing and tail feathers. Chicken or guinea feathers will do well. These may be dyed or left natural.

Remove wire from body. Make legs from chenille or small wire and insert into body. Mount birds on driftwood or a tree limb. Paint the bird bill yellow and the eye black.

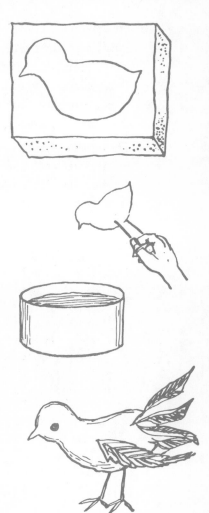

JEWELRY CHEST

Materials:

Cigar box
Different shapes of macaroni and noodles
Black enamel
Gold spray paint
Glue
Black felt

Procedure:

Paint cigar box with black enamel. When this is dry, glue on different shapes of macaroni and noodles to form a design. Turn box upside down with the lid open so it extends outward. Cover the box part with an old newspaper and spray the lid with gold paint.

The inside of the box may be painted. Cut a piece of black felt the size of the bottom of the box. Glue this in the bottom of your jewelry chest. If desired, the entire chest may be lined with the felt or other material.

PAINT BOX

GLUE ON MACARONI DESIGN

SPRAY LID WITH GOLD PAINT

PLASTIC BOBBIN PLAQUE

Materials:

Plastic bobbin (the kind lace is wound on in stores)
Black felt
Permanent foliage or small flowers
Berries
Small ceramic figure such as a pixy
Glue
Small bone ring
Gold spray paint
Small wire

Procedure:

Ask some store to save some of their plastic bobbins for you. They usually come in bright colors, but can be sprayed with gold paint.

Cut a piece of felt to fit the back of your bobbin. Cut a strip half an inch wide and an inch and a half long from the felt. Insert this through a bone ring and fold in half. Sew this to the center of the other piece of felt you have cut.

Spray the plastic bobbin with gold paint.

When this is dry, wire foliage and berries down one side of your plaque and across the bottom. Also wire a small figure, such as a pixy, to the righthand side. This will help balance your plaque as well as add interest.

Glue felt to the back of your plaque. The black and gold gives an interesting contrast.

Other plaques can be made by using one color of felt on the back and adding a figure of another color of felt on the front. Try red felt on the back and glue a green Christmas tree on the front. Bone rings covered with glue and dipped in glitter will add color to the tree. Sequins could be used in place of the bone rings.

HANDLE

CUT BACKING FROM FELT

WIRE ON
BERRIES
AND
FOLIAGE

BUTTERFLY PINCUSHION

Materials:

Cardboard

Colorful fabric

Green styrofoam (about 6 inches long and 1 inch thick)

Two buttons

Pipe cleaners

Pins

Glue

Scissors

Knife

Procedure:

Make a pattern of a butterfly from paper. Make the wing-spread seven inches. Using the paper pattern, cut one set of wings from cardboard and another set from fabric.

Punch two holes in the center of the cardboard wings. Insert a pipe cleaner to make a loop on the back to be used for hanging.

Cover the cardboard wings well with glue and place the fabric wings on this. Pull the fabric to the edge of the cardboard to remove any wrinkles.

Using a knife, cut the styrofoam into a body shape. Put glue on the underside of the body and place this on the center of the wings. From the underside insert several straight pins into the body to help hold it in place.

Glue on two buttons for eyes. Curl the ends of two pieces of pipe cleaner or colored chenille sticks. Insert one of these on each side of the butterfly's head.

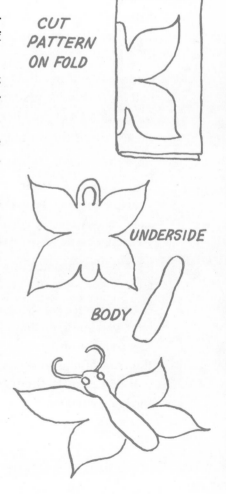

CUT PATTERN ON FOLD

UNDERSIDE

BODY

FLOWER TREE

Materials:

Cardboard cone (type used in textile mills)

Permanent flowers

Net

Straight pins

Small piece of cardboard (four inches square)

Dessert dish

Ice pick

Glue

Gold spray paint

Procedure:

Cut a circle from cardboard to fit the bottom of the cone. Glue the cardboard circle to the end of the cone.

Glue the cone to an inverted dessert dish. Spray the dish and cone with gold paint.

Punch the holes for flowers with an ice pick. Punch only a few holes at a time so that you can space your flowers well. Begin at the lower edge of the cone and continue to insert the flowers until the cone is covered. The stems of the flowers should be cut to an inch in length before inserting them in the cone.

Cut the net into two-inch squares and some in three-inch squares. The smaller squares should be used from the middle up, and the larger ones nearer the bottom. Gather the squares of net in your hands and insert a pin in the center.

Using a thimble, push the pin into the cardboard cone. Fill in all the spaces between the flowers with net.

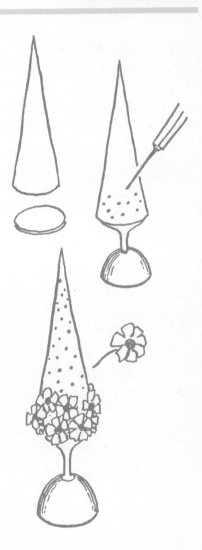

SALT AND PEPPER SHAKERS

Materials:

Two eggshells
Large wooden spool
Coping saw
Vise
Knife
Ice pick
Enamel (white, black, and red)
Small paintbrush
Two small corks
Glue

Procedure:

Select two eggs of the same size and shape. Using an ice pick, tap the center of the large end of the egg gently until the shell is pierced. In the same manner make about five more small holes around the tip of the egg.

Using the ice pick, make a larger hole in the bottom of the egg. Insert the ice pick to break the yolk. Holding the egg over a bowl, shake it until all the contents are out. (If the yolk does not shake out, blow on the end with the smaller holes.)

The bases are made by sawing a large spool in half. A vise is helpful in holding the spool in place while you saw it.

The top of the bases will need to be hollowed out so the end of the eggs will fit into them. Use a pocket knife to carve out the top of the bases. Using the knife, enlarge the holes in the spool bases so the corks will fit.

Glue the eggshells to the bases. Paint the eggs and bases with white enamel. When this is dry, paint the hair and face features. On the bases paint "salt" on one and "pepper" on the other. (If paint gets into the holes in the top of the eggs, remove it by inserting a needle through each hole.)

DIGEST DOLLY DOORSTOP

Materials:

Reader's Digest or other small magazine
Heavy cardboard
Cotton
Felt (pink, black, white, and red)
Fabric
Half a yard of ribbon
Two small bone rings or buttons (for earrings)
Three buttons
Four paper brads
Scissors
Needle and thread

Procedure:

Cut the doll from heavy cardboard.

Cover the doll form from the waist up with cotton. Wrap this with thread to hold the cotton in place.

Cut the head and hands from pink felt. Cut these half an inch larger than the cardboard form. Place on the cotton-covered cardboard and pull the felt to the back, then sew the edges together.

Cut the waist from gingham or other fabric. Make this half an inch larger than the cardboard form. Pull the edges to the back and sew in place. Sew three buttons down the waist front. As you attach the waist, you will need to turn in a small hem at the neck and at the bottom of the sleeves.

Cut a bandanna from the same fabric as used for the waist. Sew this in place at the top, turning in a hem at the lower edge.

Cut the face features from felt and glue them in place. Sew a bone ring on each side of the bandanna for earrings. Wrap some yarn on your finger, then slip it off and sew it to the center of the bandanna for hair.

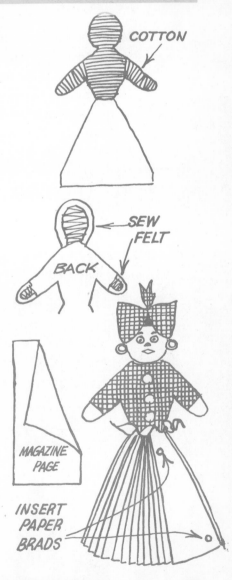

DIGEST DOLLY DOORSTOP   *(Continued)*

Make the skirt by folding pages of a small magazine such as the Reader's Digest. Begin at the front of the magazine and fold each page as shown in the diagram. When you have folded all the pages, attach the magazine to the doll form. Turn about eight pages from the front, and holding this on the doll, punch a hole at the upper part and one near the bottom all the way through the cardboard. Insert paper brads in the holes and spread the ends to hold the magazine skirt in place. Do the other side in the same manner to hold it in place.

Gather the ribbon and sew it at the doll's waist.

You may wish to spray the magazine skirt with gold or other color paint before attaching it to the doll.

SNOWMAN

Materials:

Large light bulb
Two white plastic spoons
Felt (black and red)
Old white sock
Cotton
Needle and thread
Glue
Ring of Christmas greenery

Procedure:

Cut the foot from an old white sock. Insert the light bulb and tie at the lower end.

Stuff the upper portion of the sock with cotton to make the head.

Tie at the top and around the neck.

Sew the spoons to the sock at the back of the snowman.

Make a vest of red felt and a hat of black felt. Glue black circles of felt on the body for buttons. Glue a red band on the hat.

Set your snowman in a circle of greenery or flowers.

(Since a glass bulb is used in this project, it is not recommended for children.)

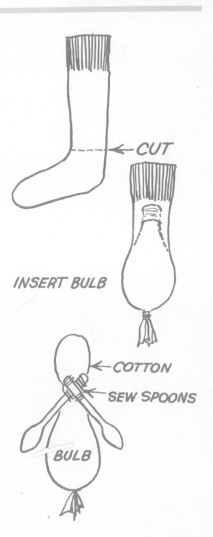

CUT

INSERT BULB

COTTON

SEW SPOONS

BULB